Airbnb Entrepreneur

How to Run Your Own Successful Short-Term Rental Enterprise

Table of Contents

Chapter 1. Introduction

In this exciting Special Report, we unlock the doors to a realm of opportunity with "Airbnb Entrepreneur: How to Run Your Own Successful Short-Term Rental Enterprise". This roller coaster of a read is not just a report, it's an adventure that guides you through unexplored territories of entrepreneurship enriched with nuggets of wisdom and practical step-by-step formulae. The good news: you don't need a PhD or a tech-nerd to start your journey. All you need is an eager mind ready to learn, and this user-friendly guidebook to turn your spare space into something truly special. So, brace yourself as we dive deep into the dynamic world of Airbnb hosting and transform you into a thriving entrepreneur in no time. Get ready to exceed your own expectations!

Chapter 2. Discovering Opportunities in the Airbnb Landscape

Airbnb's global reach offers unique opportunities for anyone looking to tap into the world of short-term property rentals. Whether you're an experienced landlord, or a homeowner with a spare room to let, Airbnb allows you to reach a large market of potential guests from across the world. Adapting to this platform presents an opportunity to maximize occupancy and yield higher returns on your investment. However, successful Airbnb entrepreneurship requires more than just listing a property. It requires a keen understanding of the marketplace, effective strategic planning, a focused customer service, and constant learning from experiences.

2.1. Understanding the Airbnb Marketplace

The basis for success in any venture starts with understanding the field of operation, and Airbnb is no exception. Airbnb operates as an online marketplace that connects people who want to rent out their properties (hosts) with people who are looking for accommodations (guests). Typically, the company does not own any of the listed properties. Instead, it profits by receiving commission from each booking.

Deciphering the dynamics in the Airbnb landscape begins with appreciating the thriving sharing economy. The growth of the sharing economy in recent years has majorly been fueled by technological advancements that make sharing assets cheaper and easier than ever—it's often only a click or two away. Airbnb, Uber, and TaskRabbit are among those firms that have capitalized on this phenomenon.

To understand where you fit in the marketplace, it's important to examine the competition and see what they're offering. Review the listings in your local area to understand the pricing models, the amenities that are commonly offered, minimum staying periods, guest evaluations, et cetera. When you have a solid grasp of what works well and what doesn't, you can customize your offerings to suit what potential tenants would want.

2.2. Identifying Lucrative Locations

Location is everything. It's one key factor that can potentially make or break your Airbnb business. The geographical location of a property affects the number of bookings and the rate you can charge per night. Due to this, accurate location targeting is essential.

Highly populated urban areas or places with touristic appeal typically have high demand for Airbnb rentals. They are also areas where people often feel like they don't have enough access to traditional accommodation options, hence may be willing to explore other options such as vacation rentals.

Another imperative aspect to consider when selecting a location is the legal landscape. Various cities have different rules and regulations in regard to short-term rentals. Some locations have certain restrictions or even prohibit vacation rentals, and running foul of these regulations can create significant problems. Therefore, it is vital to understand and follow all the regional laws and guidelines governing short-term rentals in your city of operation.

2.3. Market Segmentation and Positioning

Knowing your target market is vital to being successful as an Airbnb host. Your target market will impact everything—from how you set up and market your listing, to how you communicate with potential guests. People have different travel styles, budgets, and purposes for their trip. This is referred to as market segmentation.

Typically, there are three types of Airbnb guests: tourists, business travelers, and locals. Understand what type of guests will be visiting your area and tailor your home to meet their needs. For example, a property in a business hub might attract more corporate travelers and therefore, a host might want to ensure that the space offers a conducive environment for work, such as high-speed internet, a quiet room, and a dedicated workspace.

Positioning your property involves aligning your offering to meet the needs of the chosen target market, making it an attractive choice for potential guests compared to other properties in the area. A well-positioned property will be unique and unforgettable. Whether you're offering an experience of living like a local, a retreat in natural surroundings, or luxury vibes in a city penthouse, your property should ideally exude an appeal that's unique and caters to the needs of your target audience.

2.4. The Art of Pricing

Pricing is an essential part of your Airbnb business. It's a delicate balance of charging enough to make a worthwhile profit while also remaining competitive in the market. Analyze your competitive landscape, understand the pricing trends, keep an eye on seasonality, and consider the value you offer when setting your prices.

Dynamic pricing, a practice where the price changes based on supply and demand, can be a great tool for hosts. When demand is low, lower your prices slightly to attract bookings. When demand is high (peak tourism season, big events, or weekends), don't be afraid to increase your rate.

2.5. Setting Regulations and Developing Policies

Having clear house rules can prevent misunderstandings and potential conflicts with your guests. They also serve as a reference point for guests to understand what is and isn't allowed during their stay. This could include rules about smoking, pets, parties, noise, or any other limitations you want to place on guests' behavior.

Additionally, you must decide on your cancellation policy. Airbnb provides multiple cancellation options from flexible (full refund up to 1 day before arrival) to super strict (50% refund up until 60 days before arrival). Your choice of a cancellation policy can significantly impact the likelihood of gaining or losing reservations.

2.6. Nailing the Art of Guest Communication

Gone are the days when you could just hand over the keys to your guest and be done with it. With more individuals becoming hosts, it's crucial to provide exceptional customer service. Actively communicating with guests from the time they book until the moment they check out, can solidify a positive impression of you and your property.

2.7. Harnessing Technology for Growth

It's also important to explore how technology can be harnessed to improve your Airbnb business. This could involve using property management software to help automate tasks such as calendar management, communicating with guests, or even pricing your property. Understanding the use of analytics may also help you unlock insights about your guests' booking and stay patterns, while integration with social media platforms might broaden your market reach.

2.8. Conclusion

Starting a successful Airbnb business doesn't occur by happenstance. It's the result of a calculated series of strategic plans, decisions, and actions. By understanding the Airbnb landscape, identifying opportunities, and effectively utilizing resources at your disposal, you can navigate the world of short-term rentals, and emerge a prolific entrepreneur. Regardless of the scale of your operation, the sky is the limit—once you start, there's no telling what heights you can achieve.

Chapter 3. The Legalities of Airbnb: Staying on Safe Ground

A journey of success in the Airbnb entrepreneurship first requires understanding the laws that govern this business. Short-term rentals have sprung up in many places around the world, offering unique experiences to travelers and lucrative business opportunities to owners. However, the rise of this business model has also brought legal, regulatory, and tax challenges that vary significantly by location. Intricate knowledge of these aspects will ensure that your Airbnb business starts and stays on firm footing.

3.1. Understanding Local Laws

City, county, and state laws, regulations, and rules can greatly differ when it comes to short-term rentals. Among the rules in question are zoning laws, which may prohibit rentals in certain types of buildings or zones, and housing standards that stipulate specific requirements your rental has to meet. Restrictions related to things as seemingly minor as signage may also affect your hosting unit. Additionally, many cities enforce a cap on the number of days a property can be rented each year and require a permit or license to operate.

Start by getting in touch with your local Planning or Zoning department to understand which laws and regulations apply to your property. Some municipalities have information about short-term accommodations on their websites. As rules evolve, make sure to frequently check your local government's website or consult with a locally specialized attorney to stay abreast.

3.2. Condominium and Homeowner Association Rules

If your property is part of a condominium or a homeowners association (HOA), there might be additional guidelines that apply to you. Many condos and HOAs have rules against short-term rentals, or they might require approval, additional insurance, or impose other restrictions. Violating these rules could lead to hefty fines or other penalties, so it's crucial to check the bylaws and house rules of your association before proceeding.

3.3. Lease and Other Contractual Agreements

Should you not own the property, be sure to look at your lease agreement to see whether subletting is allowed. Many rental or lease agreements prohibit subletting without the landlord's permission. Also, if your property has a mortgage or loan attached to it, the lender may have specific rules you need to follow.

3.4. Insurance Considerations

Most homeowners' insurance policies won't cover commercial activities like running a short-term rental. Neglecting to inform your insurance provider of your Airbnb hosting activities could lead to cancellation of the insurance policy and financial consequences. To cover yourself, ensure you have a suitable commercial insurance policy, which may include short-term rental insurance or a comprehensive home-sharing policy. Airbnb also offers a Host Guarantee program providing protection for up to $1 million in damages, although it shouldn't be considered a replacement for homeowners or renters insurance.

3.5. Tax Implications

You're required to report income earned from Airbnb to the tax authorities. The specifics will vary based on your country and the specifics of your operations. However, you may qualify for certain deductions. Keeping detailed records of all income and expenses related to your rental property is essential. Consult with a tax professional familiar with short-term rentals to understand your obligations.

3.6. Legal Requirements for Hosts

Depending on the jurisdiction, you may have additional legal obligations. These could include:

- Providing a safe space: As a host, you're required to ensure the safety and security of your guests. This means you must generally maintain your property, provide necessary safety equipment and security measures.
- Accessibility for people with disabilities: Some jurisdictions require accommodations to be accessible to people with disabilities. Learn about these requirements to ensure your Airbnb property is compliant.
- Protecting your guests' privacy: When installing security cameras or other recording devices, remember they must only be used in public areas like the living room or kitchen, and guests must be informed of their existence in advance.

3.7. Navigating Discrimination Laws

Airbnb has a strict non-discrimination policy, and as a host, you're required to adhere to it. The Fair Housing Act and other anti-discrimination laws might proscribe refusing service based on a protected category such as race, color, religion, sex, disability, familial status, or national origin.

Understanding the legal aspects of running an Airbnb isn't a simple task, but it's a vital part of your job as a responsible host. By making sure you're compliant with all local, state, and federal laws, you can avoid costly mistakes, fines, disputes, and maintain a reputable image in the hosting community. Speak to a competent lawyer or legal advisor if you're unsure about how to proceed – it's the safest and most responsible way to navigate the legal landscape of this exciting business opportunity.

Chapter 4. Defining Your Market: Understanding Guest Preferences

In order to establish a successful Airbnb enterprise, it's crucial to understand who your potential guests could be and what they might prefer. By understanding these specifics, you can tailor your offering to meet and exceed their expectations, resulting in higher occupancy rates, excellent reviews, and a steady stream of revenue.

4.1. Understanding Who Your Guests Are

The first step to defining your market is to comprehend who your guests are. Airbnb hosts receive guests from across the globe, varying in age, profession, and purpose of visit. If your property is located in a city center, you might attract business travelers, tourists, conference attendees, or families looking for a long weekend vacation. However, if your property is near any key attractions like popular tourist places, or natural retreats, it may bring in a completely different demographic.

To get a clearer understanding, research the people who are already visiting your area. You can utilize statistical data from the tourism industry, use insights from other local businesses, or even observe the crowds on busy days. It's essential to identify your potential guests' demographic information, like age range, occupation, income level, etc.

4.2. Tourist Peaks and Vocations

The time individuals choose to travel can also greatly impact your Airbnb business. Understanding the patterns of high and low tourist inflow in your area can help you define your market more precisely and optimize your rental prices. A good place to start could be local businesses and tourism authority websites, which often release reports or have data pertaining to visitor trends.

Take, for instance, if your area has a particular event or season that draws in a large influx of tourists; you need to be ready to tap into this surge. Carefully craft your offerings or packages to bond with the event or season. For example, if your area is known for surfing and hosts a reputable surfing competition, consider offering additional services like surfboards for rent or surfer-friendly meal packages.

4.3. Understanding Guest Preferences

Understanding guest preferences is a vital part of defining your market. This includes the kind of amenities they would prefer, the experiences they want to enjoy, and the level of service they expect from the host. Airbnb hosting goes beyond just providing a place to stay. It's about creating experiences and providing extras that can enhance your guest's stay.

For instance, a digital nomad might prefer an Airbnb equipped with strong WiFi, a comfortable workspace, and proximity to coffee shops or co-working spaces. Families, on the other hand, would appreciate child-friendly features like cribs, high chairs, safety measures, and a convenient location near parks or kid-friendly attractions.

To gather insights on guest preferences, you could conduct surveys with past guests, monitor reviews given to other Airbnb hosts in your area, or directly ask potential guests through community forums or social media.

4.4. Differentiating Your Offering

Once you've identified your potential guests and their preferences, the next step is to revise your offerings to differentiate them from the competition. This can include anything from simple additions like providing a local delicacies welcome basket, organizing city tours, or even re-designing your space to cater to a certain type of guest.

To successfully differentiate your offerings, observe what your competitors are doing, and how can you add more value. This competitive analysis will help you identify gaps that you could fill to stand out from the crowd.

4.5. Setting Appropriate Rates

Appropriate pricing is crucial to attracting the right guests to your Airbnb. Too high, and you risk turning away potential guests; too low, and you might attract guests who don't value your offering or don't meet your preferred guest profile.

To establish an optimum price, consider factors like your area's average rental price, your upkeep costs, additional services you offer, and the kind of guests you are targeting. If your Airbnb provides a premium experience compared to your competitors, a slightly higher pricing can reflect that.

Defining your market in Airbnb hosting is all about understanding your potential guests - who they are, their traveling trends, their preferences, and what they value in a short-term rental. By tailoring your offerings and pricing to meet these preferences, you are on your way to establishing a successful Airbnb enterprise. Remember, Airbnb success lies not just in house renting but creating a perfect blend of experience, comfort, and value for your guests.

Chapter 5. Property Management Essentials for Attracting Guests

Understanding the nuances of property management is pivotal to your success as an Airbnb host. Embrace this chapter as your compass navigating you through the most essential aspects of property management strategically designed to entice guests.

5.1. Making your Property Stand Out

It's a highly competitive market out there, and standing out from the crowd can make a world of difference. So, how do you get your property to beguile potential guests? The answer is simple yet profound: Attention to detail.

The first impression of your property that potential guests will have will be through your listings. High-quality, professional photographs of a clean and aesthetically pleasing space can sky-rocket your attractiveness. Use photographs effectively to highlight unique attributes of your property such as a breathtaking view, a stylish décor theme or a unique architectural feature. Avoid misleading photos and over-editing as authenticity is highly valued in the Airbnb community.

A catchy title and a detailed yet concise property description can act as magnets drawing guests to your listing. Explain what your property offers. Does it have a rustic charm? Is it uber-modern? Is it located in the heart of the city or nestled in serene nature? Be descriptive but precise. Your potential guests should be able to visualize their stay.

5.2. Stellar Housekeeping Practices

Cleanliness is paramount. A space that is spotlessly clean and smells fresh and pleasant is immediately inviting. Standardize a rigorous cleaning protocol. Take advantage of the rich resource of Airbnb's own Cleaning Handbook and the much acclaimed five-step cleaning process for guidance.

Pay attention to the small things like making sure all lights are working, cutlery is spotless, linens are crisp and fresh smelling. Make it comfortable, cozy, and welcoming while maintaining a high standard of cleanliness.

5.3. 24/7 Availability and Phenomenal Communication

Being available, approachable and friendly can help put potential guests at ease. Enable a smooth line of communication and try to respond as swiftly as possible to any queries or issues. You can do this by various means - Airbnb's platform, emails, or phone calls. Make sure all instructions such as house rules, check-in and check-out procedures, and any unique quirks that your property has, are communicated clearly to avoid any confusion.

5.4. Extra Amenities for that Extra Appeal

Think about what extras you can provide that may elevate your guests' experience. Free wifi, a coffee maker, a well-stocked bookshelf, board games, local tour guide books, family-friendly amenities if you're targeting families etc. can be a great draw. If you're in a colder region, having dependable heating systems or a cozy fireplace works wonders. If you're in a hotter region, think of installing efficient cooling systems.

5.5. The Art of Pricing

With amenities and services in place, it's time to determine the right price. Airbnb's smart pricing tool is there to guide you but don't rely on it blindly. Learn about your local market, consider your expenses and remember the rule of supply and demand. An underpriced property can often seem suspicious, and an overpriced one might lead to fewer bookings.

During peak times you may be able to charge a premium, but during the low seasons, you might want to consider lowering the price or offering discounts for extended stays. Honesty about pricing, fees, and rules regarding cancellations or damage is appreciated and cultivates trust within your audience.

5.6. Handling Guest Reviews

Guest reviews act as a passport into the experiences you offer. Strive for positive reviews as they greatly impact your visibility and subsequent bookings on Airbnb. Dealing with negative feedback with grace, understanding, and improvement is an art that can be learned. Replies to reviews should be polite, professional, and non-defensive.

5.7. Legalities and Insurance

Being well-versed in the local laws and regulations concerning short-term rentals is important. From zoning laws, housing laws, to tax obligations, ensure you've covered all bases. Additionally, consider purchasing a suitable insurance policy. Airbnb offers a host guarantee program, but this should not be viewed as a replacement for insurance.

5.8. Maintenance and Frequent Inspections

Regular maintenance and inspections can save you from potential disasters in the long run. Keeping tabs on your inventory, checking for any wear and tear, ensuring all appliances are operational, winterizing the property before winter if you're in a colder region, are all good practices to follow.

In conclusion, property management requires a multifaceted approach. By blending efficient management with the creation of a unique, inviting space that offers value for money, you can create not just an attractive listing, but memorable experiences for your guests. And in the end, that is the true essence of a successful Airbnb business. Adventure awaits you, so go forth and conquer, one guest at a time.

Chapter 6. Interior Design and Functionality: The Art of Creating Amazing Spaces

Designing your Airbnb property involves a mix of creativity and strategy. It's critical to balance stunning aesthetics with tried-and-true functionality in order to create a guest experience that results in glowing reviews and repeat visitors. To assist you in navigating through this exciting process, we'll break the process into digestible pieces, examining each aspect minutely.

6.1. Getting Started With a Vision

Crafting the perfect space for your Airbnb starts with developing an overarching vision for your place. Consider what type of visitor you're trying to attract and what kind of experience you want to offer. Are you aiming towards luxury-seekers or budget adventurers? Whether cozy farmhouse charm or sleek minimalist design is your aim, having a vision helps guide your decisions as you design and decorate.

6.2. Importance of Consistency

Consistency is not just a design principle, but a hallmark of professionalism. From your Airbnb listing photos to the actual guest experience, maintaining a consistent theme and vibe throughout your property builds trust with visitors.

6.3. Crafting a Color Palette

Your chosen color palette can dramatically affect the mood and perceived space within your home. Light, neutral colors can make a small room feel larger and more open, while bold, rich colors can make a large room feel cozy and inviting. A careful consideration of the placement, size, and amount of color is crucial.

6.4. Prioritizing Comfort

Comfort should be at the top of your priority list when outfitting your Airbnb property. Guests may forgive a less-than-perfect color scheme, but a lumpy mattress or a lack of seating space will likely cost you in the reviews department. Spend a bit extra on quality mattresses, high thread-count sheets, plush towels, and comfortable seating.

6.5. Optimizing for Functionality

Think about the practical aspects of life in your rental property. Is there ample lighting and accessible outlets? Is the kitchen stocked with cooking supplies for nights when guests prefer to stay in? Special attention should be given to making sure all corners of your Airbnb serve a specific, functional purpose.

6.6. A Note on Personal Touches

Personal touches, such as a welcome basket with local goodies or a hand-written note, can make all the difference in helping guests feel welcome and cared-for. Another idea would be to integrate elements of local culture or traditions in your decor, offering guests a unique and immersive experience.

6.7. Accessories: The Final Touches

This final aspect of your interior design vision is the use of accessories. These are items - such as throw pillows, rugs, curtains, art, lamps, and other decor items - that bring color, texture, and personality to your space. This is your chance to add those final layers of comfort and charm that truly make your property feel like a home away from home.

Remember, like any great enterprise, designing the perfect Airbnb space is a journey. It takes time, patience, and continual refinement, but when your efforts culminate in a stellar guest experience, you'll realize it was well worth it. At the end of the day, you're not just creating spaces, you're crafting experiences.

Chapter 7. Customer Service Excellence: Nurturing Positive Guest Experiences

Achieving Customer Service Excellence in your Airbnb enterprise involves a buffet of skills, including – but not limited to - active listening, problem-solving, responsiveness and anticipation of guest needs. It all starts with making a positive first impression, followed by consistently building upon that impression throughout your guest's stay.

7.1. The Importance of First Impressions

The first impression you make on your guests can set the tone for the rest of their stay. Are your listing descriptions accurate and enticing? Are your photos clear and representative of the space? Is your place properly cleaned before your guests' arrival? Remember that these 'firsts' are also a reflection of your attitude and work ethic as a host.

7.2. Communication is Key

Clear, timely, and concise communication plays a pivotal role in taking your customer service from good to great. Start with a friendly welcome message congratulating your guest on their booking and sharing relevant check-in details. Keep communication channels open during their stay, promptly responding to any questions or issues they may have. Always be available, however, respect your guests' privacy as well.

7.3. Furnishing the Perfect Airbnb

What kind of experience do you want to provide your guests? This question will guide you in furnishing and styling your Airbnb. A guest's comfort should be your top priority when choosing furniture. Offer a well-equipped kitchen, clean washrooms with enough supplies, comfortable beds, and fast internet. Quirky additions, like board games or a bookshelf, can make their stay even more memorable.

7.4. Anticipate Guest Needs

Anticipating your guests' needs goes a long way in enhancing their experience. Are you providing all the basics – toiletries, kitchen essentials, extra bedding and towels – plus maybe a local city guide or a list of favorite nearby restaurants? Adding personal touches, like welcome baskets with local goodies, can leave a lasting impression.

7.5. Handling Guest Complaints and Issues

Even with the best intentions and careful planning, issues can arise. A quick, flexible, and positive response to problems is essential. Develop a comprehensive list of local maintenance contacts – plumbers, electricians, locksmiths – to tackle any emerging technical issues. If guests voice complaints, listen, apologize, rectify, and, if applicable, compensate. This shows that you're committed to ensuring a pleasant stay for all your guests.

7.6. Collecting and Responding to Feedback

Feedback is crucial for improvement. Encourage guests to leave a review and be sure to respond to each one – both positive and negative. Complimenting positive feedback can encourage repeat business. For negative feedback, apologize and take responsibility, but also use this as an opportunity to recognize areas for improvement.

7.7. Learning from the Best: Case Studies of Successful Hosts

One of the best ways to learn the ropes of any industry is to study those who are doing it successfully. This could involve reading up on case studies, participating in host community forums, or even reaching out directly to successful hosts for advice. Note their best practices and determine how you can incorporate similar strategies in your own Airbnb enterprise.

7.8. Maintaining Consistent Standards

Once you've established what works best in your Airbnb, consistency is key. Whether it's the quality of your listing, the cleanliness of your property, the amenities you provide, or your promptness in responding to queries - strive to maintain and elevate the standards you have set.

Overall, customer service in the short-term rental industry is truly about showing you care. From the initial interaction to the farewell message, hosting is a constant exercise in hosting integrity, communication, and attentive service. With a dash of dedication, a spoonful of understanding, and a big helping of going the extra mile, you'll be well on your way to Airbnb success. Pave your path to a future where your guest reviews vouch for your exemplary efforts, giving you the recognition you deserve in the vibrant universe of Airbnb hosting. A universe where you rule!

Chapter 8. Pricing Strategies: Mastering Competitive and Fair Rates

Setting a pricing strategy for your Airbnb listing is a delicate balancing act. It needs to be profitable enough to make your business viable, but competitive enough to attract guests. Therein lies your challenge: how to set up competitive and fair rates? This chapter delves into the practical strategies involved.

8.1. Understanding the Market

Before we delve into specific pricing strategies, it's important to develop a solid understanding of the market. To do that, we'll need to conduct some research. Start by getting to know your competition - other short-term rentals in your area.

Use Airbnb's search functions to see what others in your area are charging. As you do this, remember to make fair comparisons. Compare properties that offer similar amenities, in comparable locations, and are of a similar size. This will give you a baseline for what guests are willing to pay in your area.

Additionally, it's not just about the dollar amount but the value offered for that price. What amenities and services are these properties offering their guests? Free Wi-Fi? A hot tub? Proximity to popular tourist attractions? Don't just blindly copy other hosts' rates, understand what value they offer in exchange for their asking price.

8.2. On Pricing Variables

Several factors dictate your Airbnb listing's price. These variables include:

1. The season or time of year
2. The day of the week (weekday vs. weekend)
3. The type of property you're renting out
4. The unique features and amenities your property offers
5. The number of guests your property can accommodate

Every Airbnb entrepreneur should be aware of these variables and consider them in their pricing strategies. Tailoring your rates to reflect these variables can dramatically increase your occupancy rates and revenue.

8.3. A Dynamic Pricing Strategy

Airbnb allows for automatic pricing, where an algorithm adjusts your rate based on demand and supply factors. While this can be helpful in some cases, it may not always reflect the true value of your property or the fluctuations that seasonality and local events can bring.

That's why it's critical to consider a dynamic pricing strategy, where prices are adjusted regularly based on a variety of factors. This could mean sharp price increases during peak season or popular events in your area, and lower than average prices during slower times.

Using a dynamic pricing tool—some of which integrate with Airbnb—can help with this. They factor in variables like broader market demand, competitor pricing, seasonality, local events, and booking trends.

8.4. Pricing For Longer Stays

You might want to consider offering discounts for longer-term stays.

Guests planning longer vacations or work trips generally prefer locations that give them more value for their money. Offering weekly or monthly discounts not only makes your listing attractive to these guests but also helps minimize vacancies and generate a consistent income.

8.5. Easy Cancellations Equal Higher Rates

One compelling pricing strategy is to offer flexible cancellation policies. You're more likely to attract bookings if guests feel they have the freedom to cancel their trip if unexpected events occur. They're also likely to be willing to pay a tad more for that flexibility. It's a trade-off that can work well in your favor.

8.6. Fees & Extra Charges

Consideration must be given to fees such as cleaning fees, extra person fees, and the security deposit. Strategically setting these fees can significantly influence your overall revenue and your potential guests' perception of your listing's value.

Above all, transparency is key. Hidden fees can upset guests and lead to negative reviews. Always clearly list all fees and ensure the guest is aware of the total cost before they confirm their booking.

By understanding and mastering these pricing strategies, you will be in a better position to price your Airbnb listing competitively and fairly. However, it's important to remember that pricing isn't static. Continually revising your pricing in response to market trends and changes in demand is key to remaining competitive in a dynamic market like short-term rentals.

Remember, the goal is not only to attract guests but to provide excellent value that will prompt positive reviews, return guests, and referrals. Your pricing strategy can help achieve this. It's not just about what guests pay but about what they get for their payment.

In the following chapters, we will explore other aspects of running a successful short-term rental business. From creating a killer listing to providing an unmatched guest experience, this guide is your key to becoming a successful Airbnb entrepreneur!

Chapter 9. Digital Marketing for Short-Term Rentals: Enhancing Your Online Presence

Engaging with potential customers and driving traffic to your listing is crucial in short-term rentals. This requires an effective and comprehensive plan of digital marketing, where your online presence can significantly affect your rental's visibility, accessibility, influence, and consequently your revenue. This chapter provides a complete rundown on how to enhance your online presence focusing on an array of digital marketing strategies.

9.1. Understanding Digital Marketing

Digital marketing is an umbrella term for all of your online marketing efforts. To promote your Airbnb listing effectively, you should leverage web marketing assets like your website, blog content, online brochure or lookbook, social networking channels, email marketing, and even organic search engine results. Tools like Search Engine Optimization (SEO), Pay-Per-Click (PPC) advertising, content marketing, social media marketing, email marketing, and online PR can all contribute to your digital marketing strategy.

9.2. Building Your Website

One of the first steps towards effective digital marketing for your Airbnb property is to have a website of your own. This serves as a convenient platform showcasing all details about your rental.

Include clear, high-quality pictures, descriptive but concise information about the property, its features and the surrounding area. Make it easy for visitors to book directly and provide an easy way to get in touch for inquiries.

Ensure your website is designed with user experience in mind. It should be easy to navigate, fast to load, and aesthetically pleasing. By having a great user experience, you increase the chances of a viewer booking, returning for future bookings, or recommending your property to others.

9.3. SEO for Your Website

To get your website noticed organically, implement Search Engine Optimization (SEO) strategies. Research keywords related to your rental and local area and incorporate these in page titles, headings, and content. Do regular SEO audits to see where you rank on search engines, and continually optimize your content for better visibility.

9.4. Collaboration and Back-linking

Another effective SEO tactic is back-linking. When relevant websites link back to yours, it increases your site's authority. This can be achieved through guests' blogs, local businesses, travel websites, or collaborating with influencers. Inclusive, make sure to link to your website on your social media profiles to enhance visibility.

9.5. Content Marketing

Content is king in the digital marketing landscape. It can significantly increase the visibility and attractiveness of your listing. Aim to create and share valuable content that potential guests might find helpful, including city guides, recommended local attractions, or tips for traveling in your area.

You can also start a blog linked to your website, where you share stories or advice. This not only helps with SEO but also builds a connection with your audience by providing them relevant, engaging content, making them want to stay at your rental property.

9.6. Email Marketing

Establishing a customer email list and periodically sending out enticing newsletters can be incredibly powerful. The newsletters can include updates about your rental, special offers, or useful content, urging past guests to revisit and compelling new guests to book. Remember to stay GDPR compliant while collecting and storing data.

9.7. Social Media Marketing

Social media platforms are an excellent medium to engage with your potential customers. Focus on platforms where your target audience is most active—this could be Facebook, Instagram, or LinkedIn. These allow you to share updates, create engaging content like videos, behind-the-scenes images, and reviews. You can also run targeted paid ads to reach a larger audience.

9.8. Online Reviews and Reputation Management

Online reviews are incredibly influential in a user's decision-making process, particularly in a sharing economy platform like Airbnb. Encourage guests to leave written reviews and ratings after their stay. Make sure to reply sincerely to both positive and critical reviews, showing that you value your customers' feedback and are proactive about improving guest experiences.

9.9. Analytics and Performance Tracking

Finally, monitoring and tracking your progress is essential to any marketing strategy. Use tools like Google Analytics and Airbnb's own booking data information to track your website traffic, booking conversions, or the effectiveness of social media campaigns. Regularly analyzing your data will help you understand what strategies are working and need to be enhanced.

Digital marketing can seem daunting, but with these tips and tools, you're well on your way to boosting your short-term rental's online presence and, ultimately, your success.

It's time to start tailoring these tactics to your business, considering your budget, goals, target audience, and resources available. Remember that consistency and patience are crucial—digital marketing efforts often take time to mature, but their benefits can be substantial and long-lasting. Keep learning, adapting, and evolving in your journey as a successful Airbnb entrepreneur!

Chapter 10. Growth and Scaling: Expanding Your Airbnb Empire

Congratulations on making it this far into your Airbnb journey. By now, you should have a solid understanding of the skills and resources required to run your own successful short-term rental business. But like any property venture, there's always room for growth and expansion.

However, it's not just about adding more properties to your portfolio. It's also about optimizing your existing operations to boost your ROI.

10.1. Understanding the Growth Horizons

Growth in property management is often mistakenly perceived as simply the acquisition of more properties. While this is indeed a route to scaling, it's crucial to understand the other dimensions of growth as well - performance optimization and diversification.

Performance optimization means getting more revenue out of your existing properties. This could be through increasing your occupancy rate, increasing your nightly rate, providing add-on services, or any combination thereof.

Diversification, on the other hand, refers to adding different types of properties to your portfolio. If you currently own and rent apartments, for example, considering options like Houses, Condos, or even unique stays like Treehouses, Barns, etc., extends the appeal and reach of your Airbnb enterprise.

Understanding these two types of growth will enable you to develop a growth strategy that aligns with your goals and resources.

10.2. Formulating a Growth Strategy

Now, let's talk strategy. In order to succeed in the competitive Airbnb market, you'll need to have a robust strategy in place. Here are things to consider:

- Target market - Continue to refine the demographic you intend to attract. Demographics can be based on age, interests, the purpose of travel, etc.
- Competitive analysis - understand other successful hosts in your area and the kind of properties they offer. Identify what they're doing right and adopt relevant strategies.
- Pricing strategy - This should be dynamic, adjusting to changes in demand and competition.
- Operational efficiency - Designed to reduce friction and ensure a seamless experience for your guests, thereby freeing up your time to focus on expansion.

10.3. Financing Your Expansion

Acquiring new properties is a big step and usually requires substantial capital. However, there are multiple ways in which you can finance your expansion:

- Traditional Mortgage - This is the most common method of financing the purchase of additional properties.
- Home Equity Line of Credit (HELOC) - Allows you to borrow against the equity in your existing property (ies).
- Partnerships - Teaming up with investors who have the required capital but lack the time or expertise to manage short-term

rentals can be a win-win partnership.

Remember, each financing method comes with its own risks and benefits. So, make a truly informed decision rather than jumping right in.

10.4. Scaling Your Operations

When it comes to scale, automation, and delegation are your best allies. Ideally, you want to progressively remove yourself from day-to-day property management.

Automation could be in the form of using Airbnb's smart pricing tool, auto-responses for inquiry messages, or automatically syncing your calendar across multiple listing sites.

Scaling can also involve delegation. Hiring a reliable property manager, virtual assistant, or a cleaning service can free up your time for more strategic pursuits.

As your Airbnb empire expands, continually reassess your operations and refine the processes that allow you to maintain high standards and efficient workflows.

10.5. Coping with Regulatory Changes

A final consideration in your growth agenda should involve regulatory requirements. As your business expands, so too will the regulatory landscape change, depending on the locations you operate in.

Understand the zoning laws, tax implications, and other legal requirements of your chosen area, and plan accordingly to ensure compliance while leveraging the best possible opportunities.

Scaling your Airbnb enterprise is an exciting adventure. It requires careful planning, focus, commitment, and, at times, a dose of healthy risk-taking. Bear in mind, every growth step is a learning opportunity. Make your moves with confidence, refine strategies as needed, and usher in a new era of growth and prosperity for your Airbnb venture.

Chapter 11. Overcoming Challenges: From Hurdles to Success in the Airbnb Enterprise

The first step in building your successful Airbnb enterprise is recognizing that challenges are an inherent part of the journey. But don't fret - these challenges should not discourage you. Instead, they should fuel your drive to create a better, stronger enterprise.

11.1. Identifying Your Challenges

Every Airbnb host will encounter their unique set of challenges. Some problems may be big and complex, requiring a comprehensive strategy to overcome. Others would need only quick fixes. The key lies in quickly identifying what these challenges are, and swiftly finding the right solution for them.

11.1.1. Market Analysis

Understanding your market is crucial in running any business, more so for an Airbnb enterprise. It might be tempting to just dive in, list your property, and expect bookings to roll in. However, without proper market analysis, you're practically navigating in the dark.

- Who is your ideal guest?
- What attributes of your property would appeal to them?
- How does your competition perform?
- What's the optimal pricing strategy?
- Which amenities are essential, and which are just nice-to-have?

Make sure to conduct a thorough market analysis before jumping in and you will be pleasantly surprised by the impact it has on your bottom line.

11.1.2. Rules and Regulations

Navigating through the maze of local laws, zoning ordinances, and HOA rules can be daunting. Failing to do so, though, could lead to steep fines or even having your Airbnb enterprise shut down. It's therefore crucial that you're fully aware of the regulations in your area before you start your venture. Consider consulting with a lawyer or a local regulatory board to help you fully comprehend the laws that could affect your hosting.

11.1.3. Taxes, Insurance, and Financial Planning

Sorting out your finances may not be the most exciting part of being an Airbnb host, but it's absolutely critical. Every host should have a clear understanding of how Airbnb income affects their tax situation. You should also have an insurance coverage strategy in place to protect yourself from any liabilities. And finally, it's important to consider all aspects of financial planning.

11.2. Mastering Your Challenges

Once you've identified your challenges it is time to move past them. This involves meticulous planning, being adaptable, learning from your mistakes, and never being afraid to seek help when needed.

11.2.1. Crafting a Comprehensive Hosting Strategy

Start by crafting a comprehensive hosting strategy that covers all the basics of hosting –from pricing and amenities to guest communication and reviews. This will be your 'business plan' outlining how you wish to execute your hosting and how to effectively deal with the daily challenges of managing a property.

11.2.2. Embrace the Agile Approach

Running an Airbnb enterprise is not a static, one-size-fits-all operation. Just as every host is unique, so too will be their set of challenges and solutions. The key to success here is staying flexible and constantly assessing your approach. Experiment with different strategies for issues like pricing and guest communication. Keep what works, change what doesn't.

11.2.3. Learn from Every Misstep

Every challenge you face is a learning opportunity. Even negative reviews can be blessings in disguise. Approach each adversity with an open mind and a resolution to learn and it will soon feel like no hurdle is too high to overcome.

11.2.4. Tap Into the Airbnb Community

Remember you're not alone - you're part of a global community of Airbnb hosts. They are your richest resource. Reach out to fellow hosts through Airbnb's community forum, networking events or online communities dedicated to Airbnb hosts.

11.3. Realizing Your Success

Overcoming challenges might be tough, but it's the only way to success. Realize that success doesn't come overnight - it comes through persistent, consistent effort and a commitment to improvement.

11.3.1. Celebrate Small Victories

Every alleviated guest concern, every five-star review, every month of strong bookings, these are all cause for celebration. Celebrate these wins and remember them as you march ahead.

11.3.2. Keep Optmizing, Keep Improving

After overcoming a hurdle, a successful Airbnb host doesn't just stop there - they optimize, they refine, they strive for further improvement. Keep revisiting your strategies, keep refining your plans, and keep striving for excellence.

By identifying the challenges, mastering them with strategic planning and agility, and continually improving and optimizing, you will not just survive in the Airbnb marketplace, but thrive. Embrace these philosophies, and put them into action. Soon, your Airbnb enterprise's success will be not just a possibility, but a reality.

www.ingramcontent.com/pod-product-compliance
Lightning Source LLC
Chambersburg PA
CBHW071548030426
42412CB00022B/155
9798856604541